Dumfries and Galloway

Through the Lens
Glimpses of old
Kirkbean and Southwick

GW00392504

Dumfries and Galloway
Libraries, Information and Archives
2002

Designed by Dumfries and Galloway Libraries, Information
and Archives. Set and printed by Solway Offset Services,
Catherinefield Industrial Estate, Dumfries for the publisher.

Dumfries and Galloway Libraries, Information and Archives
Central Support Unit, Catherine Street
Dumfries DG1 1JB
Tel: 01387 252070   Fax: 01387 260294
www.dumgal.gov.uk/lia

ISBN 0 946280 55 X
Kirkbean and Southwick is number 21 in the
Dumfries and Galloway: Through the Lens series.
For a full list of our publications contact us at the above address.

ACKNOWLEDGEMENTS

A Truckell, N Clark, K Clark, T Clark, R
Pickering, A Rook, B McCormick, H Barbour,
J McMyn, A Carson, J Kirkland, R Morland,
B Blackett, G Fazakerley, Southerness Golf
Club.

INTRODUCTION

The area covered by this book comprises the parish of Kirkbean and the ancient parish of Southwick. The later merged with that of Colvend to the west in 1612, but was more closely linked in many ways to the east and Kirkbean. Sheltered by the bulk of Criffel and its neighbouring hills, the coastal strip is moist and mild in climate with fertile alluvial soils, and has been called the Garden of Galloway. It is certainly of unusual beauty. The countryside, and the settlements of Kirkbean, Carsethorn, Caulkerbush and Mainsriddle, have changed little over the past hundred years, with only a scattered sprinkling of new buildings. It is rather the economic and social fabric that has altered.

In 1900 Kirkbean parish and Southwick belonged almost wholly to the three estates of Arbigland, Cavens and Southwick; the large majority of the population worked on their land, and many others on the sea, in the coasting trade and on shrimping boats. Even by 1950 only 30 out of a population of 548 worked outside the parish. Today, both ownership and employment patterns have shifted radically. Farms are owner-occupied, the regular agricultural workforce is very small and many houses are owned by retired people, commuters or as second homes. The boom in tourism has resulted in the one great expansion in the area; that of Southerness. Since the Second World War the promontory ending in Southerness Point has become home to an ever-increasing range of leisure facilities, from caravans and huts to golf courses and most recently, the new RSPB Reserve at Mersehead Farm.

This collection of photographs could not have been assembled without the generosity of local people. Acknowledgements are given on the opposite page, but special thanks are due to Ralph Pickering, who had the original idea for the book and who collected nearly all the material for it, and to Jim Kirkland, who kindly and patiently saw the publishing process through to conclusion.

CARSETHORN JETTY
This fine view of about 1900 shows the old jetty with shrimping or fishing boat moored off it and their nets out to dry. The two well-dressed ladies in the foreground, seated on a punt or rowing boat, are possibly engaged in dressmaking. On the far left are the bows of the *Scotia* (see p. 38).

CLARK'S BUS AT SOUTHERNESS
The Clark family ran a service from Southerness to Dumfries between early 1900s to 1949, graduating from a horse drawn vehicle to motorised buses and based at what became the John Paul Jones Hotel. Bill Clark is the driver pictured and the bus is an Albion.

DRUMBURN SAWMILL
The mill was situated a hundred yards or so west of the hamlet, but is now demolished. Bob Stitt is seen here with Jack Purdie. The Carsethorn lifeboat "Georgina Frances," donated about 1890 by Colonel and Mrs Blackett, is in for its summer refit.

FLOODING AT KIRKBEAN
On 27th June 1998 an unexpected flash flood engulfed Kirkbean village. The water, over three feet deep, was beginning to carry the car belonging to Joe Shepherd away; Nigel Wallace and Jim Wilson are seen attaching a tow rope to anchor it.

HOUSE ON THE SHORE

The picture shows the house under construction in about 1935. The wing in the foreground is on the site of Gardenfoot Cottage, previously occupied by the Head Gardener of Arbigland, Mr Houliston. The House on the Shore was built for £2,000 and much of the stone came from disused cottages at Slate Row, Carsethorn.

DUKES STREET, KIRKBEAN

This row of Cavens Estate Cottages has become known as Dukes Street. The gable at the end of the row is Burnside, the cottage so badly flooded in 1998. The house by the bridge is known as Crockadobly. Behind the street was a wooden house built on stilts, occupied for many years by the King family.

KIRKBEAN CHURCH

The church designed by William Craik of Arbigland was built on the site of an earlier church in 1776 and cost £365. The cupola which gives the building its unique character was designed by the Dumfries architect Walter Newall in about 1835; his parents lived for some years at Airdrie Farm. The war memorial was unveiled in 1921 and paid for by local subscriptions, and the gate pillars to its left have memorial plaques to those who served in and survived the Great War. This photograph was taken shortly after the memorial was built in July 1921.

ROBSON SISTERS, CARSETHORN
The sisters, shown here in their Sunday best, were from left to right Elizabeth, Agnes and Mary. The latter was Mr Alfie Truckell's mother. The girls are pictured in Kirkbean Glen, a popular walk at this time, the early 1900s. The ground was maintained by the Cavens Estate.

KIRKBEAN VILLAGE

This photograph was taken around 1908 from behind Woodside House. The smithy was the right-hand part of the pair of cottages on the far right; in the left distance is the manse. In the near foreground is the roof of the Cavens Estate Office and the foremost right of the cottages in the centre foreground housed the village Library and Reading Room.

ROAD ROLLER

The steam roller seen here at East Preston Farm in the 1960s was the last one working in the South West of Scotland. A feature of the road-making and mending scene for more than 50 years, they are still to be seen in pristine condition at vintage machinery shows.

DRUMBURN DELIVERY

Drumburn, like many of the local houses, had a cellar for storing the proceeds of the smuggling trade; in the eighteenth century the trade, in particular with the Isle of Man, used many local harbours and inlets. This photograph was taken in the early 1960s, and shows the well-known delivery van of McMichael's the Bakers of Lochmaben, one of the many supplying rural areas in a time of limited car ownership.

MR and MRS MCCORMICK, POWILLIMOUNT COTTAGES
Mr and Mrs Tom McCormick outside their cottage at Powillimount. Tom was a ploughman, ditcher and drainer on Arbigland Estate and two of their eight sons were also employed on the Estate. Mrs McCormick died in 2001 just short of her century.

MARY STITT
Seen here in 1943, in the uniform of the Land Girls, Mary came from Glasgow to Kirkhouse, Kirkbean in the Second World War and married Will Stitt, Joiner of Drumburn. The Second World War saw the most drastic short-term changes to rural life in recent centuries; the influx of evacuees and prisoners-of-war (some of the latter were also living at Kirkhouse), together with city women like Mary Stitt working on the land, meant that life would never be quite the same again for any of them.

HARROWING AT NEWMAINS
In the third Statistical Account for Kirkbean Parish written by Rev. A. Dickson in 1952 he stated that *Farming has of course became highly mechanised and the oil-driven tractor has taken the place of the horse.* This is maybe a reason why this photograph, of David McFadyean harrowing at Newmains Farm in the early 1950s, was taken; in many parishes tractors outnumbered horses by this date, and some folk were capturing the vanishing way of life on film.

PRESTON CROSS

The cross is the last visible remnant of the burgh of Preston, between Kirkbean and Southerness, which was founded by the Earl of Nithsdale in 1633. In the seventeenth and eighteenth centuries landowners founded many small settlements which were granted burgh status giving certain priviledges to the inhabitants in the hope that land could be feued to incomers thereby profiting the owners. The hoped for economic transformation failed to materialise, although a map of 1761 shows the *towns* of Preston and Kirkbean, which were no more than small villages.

ARBIGLAND HOUSE IN THE GREAT SNOW

In February 1996 eighteen inches of snow fell in a twenty-four hour period, the heaviest fall since 1947. Roads were blocked, trees and electricity lines were brought down and many farm buildings suffered collapsed roofs from the weight of snow. Arbigland House, the finest in the area, was built by William Craik in 1755. Craik was one of the most notable men in the Stewartry of Kirkcudbright throughout his long life, and gained particular fame as one of the first agricultural improvers. The gardens running down to the sea are now as well-known as the house.

BINDING AT NORTH CARSE

This photograph, taken in 1930s, shows a three-horse binder in operation. The bound s can be seen on the left; the crop was probably oats. North Carse Farm is in Carsethorn Village, with lands extending to the north.

THRESHING AND BALING AT NEWMAINS
This scene of intense activity in 1959 was the last of its kind at Newmains Farm. Kingan's of New Abbey were the contractors, although the tractor was owned by G & J Clark of Newmains, and was a blue Fordson Major first registered in 1958. In subsequent years the newfangled combine harvester would do the job.

COLONEL BLACKETT AT ARBIGLAND
Colonel Christopher Blackett, seated in the rear of the carriage (probably a shooting-brake) in this view of about 1900 was a Crimea Veteran who died in 1904. His wife Georgina died in 1914. The Blackett family had bought the estate from the Craiks in 1852, and were in possession of the house until 2000, when both house and contents were sold.

ARBIGLAND HOUSE, PRESENTATION
The 21st birthday presentation of C W S Blackett took place outside Arbigland House in April 1929. In the centre can be seen General Swiny and Mrs Blackett-Swiny and in the foreground, presenting the silver tea service, is the senior tenant farmer, Mr McWilliam.

PRESTON MILL, BLACKSMITH
Willie Barbour the blacksmith can be seen here shortly before his death in 1967. Unusually, the blacksmith's shop is still in operation under the ownership of Alex Seggie, although the age of the working horse has long gone. Preston Mill is a small village which grew up around the grain mill worked by the Preston Burn.

WEST PRESTON RAF BARRACKS
This view of the barracks, built in 1939, was taken from the water-tower. The barracks were built as a base for target practice which took place for fighters and bombers around the local coastline. The residents of the barracks would have monitored the results of the practice. The residents obviously dug for Victory as can be seen from the serried ranks of various vegetables growing in profusion.

NEWMAINS, BIG SNOW
This was the really big snow of 1947, which lasted for many weeks and coincided with a very cold spell. The snow in many areas rose above the level of the fence-tops, causing problems for farmers who couldn't keep their sheep on their own farms. In the foreground are snow-drifts on the Southerness road.

KIRKHOUSE FARM

The farm labourers are lined up with their working horses in this excellent view from about 1914. Kirkhouse was a 250 acre dairy farm sending milk to Glasgow during the winter months when production was low, although in the summer the milk was made into cheese. The feed was mostly hay, straw, turnips and grass, supplemented with oats and a little bran meal. The Ayrshire cows were housed in byres and milked by hand until 1918 when a Wallace (of Castle Douglas) milking machine was installed. In 2000 dairy farming ceased at Kirkhouse after over a hundred years.

KIRKBEAN VILLAGE

This view was taken in 1952, looking up the unrecognisably narrow Dumfries road. The building centre right is the Post Office, and to its right is the stable, built to house the telegraph boy's pony. The car was owned by Steve Harrison seen here leaning against it. He's talking to the local rabbit catcher.

SOUTHERNESS LIGHTHOUSE

The lighthouse, one of the most familiar sights of the Solway Coast, was first built in 1748-9 and paid for by the Town Council of Dumfries. The tower was subsequently raised twice, the second time to a design by the Dumfries architect and engineer Walter Newall between 1842 and 1844. Financial costs eventually led to the extinguishing of the light in 1867, but it was relit in 1894 by Mrs Blackett of Arbigland and only finally ceased operation in 1936. This photograph dates from about 1925; the charabanc is shuttling visitors backwards and forwards to the already popular holiday village.

SOUTHERNESS VILLAGE
In this view of about 1920 from the top of the lighthouse Southerness is not greatly altered from the village established by the Oswalds of Cavens between the 1770s and 1790s. Some cottages were built to house potential coal-miners, and then potential lime-quarriers, before the poor quality of both substances ruled out Southerness' participation in the Industrial Revolution. By the 1790s the Oswalds were promoting the village as a sea-bathing resort, foreshadowing its occupation for its history to date. Note the storm shutters on the right-foreground cottages.

SOUTHERNESS CARAVAN SITE

After the Second World War a new era dawned for the village. Mr Brown of Gillfoot sited a few caravans on his farm which extends eastwards towards Powillimount. By the date of this photograph, about 1960, the site had greatly expanded and another one, shown here, had opened closer to the village. The John Paul Jones Hotel, the large building on the far left, was in use as the Golf Clubhouse. By the mid-1970s new buildings included a food store and amusement arcade to cater for the 700 or so caravan and hut-dwellers. Fights between Glasgow and Newcastle holiday-makers were common, and caused some problems for the local Dalbeattie and Dumfries police.

SOUTHWICK CHURCH

The old church of Southwick fell out of use in the late 18th century, after the amalgamation of Southwick and Colvend parishes. The ruins still remain below the steep slopes of Clifton Craig and Laggan Hill, over a mile west of the present building. Sir Mark McTaggart Stewart of Southwick Hall, tired of the ten-mile round trip to Colvend, commissioned Peddie and Kinnear, the well-known Edinburgh architects, to design and build a new Southwick Kirk. Opened in July 1891 at a cost of nearly £3,000, it was a combination of Norman and late medieval Scottish styles, with its round-headed windows and tower with corbelled parapet and cannon-like gargoyle waterspouts. It is still widely admired today.

CAVENS HOUSE

The Oswald family's original lands were at Auchencruive near Ayr, but they purchased the estate of Cavens, in the centre of the parish and including most of what is now Kirkbean Village, in the eighteenth century. For the next couple of centuries and until recent times the family members played an important role in community life. Cavens House, a small but extended Georgian House was owned and let out or lived in by various Oswalds until about 1950, when it was sold. It is now a country house hotel.

CAULKERBUSH
Caulkerbush first appears on a map in the 1780s, when it was named on a plan showing lands the ownership of which was disputed by Sir James Riddell and the owners of the farm of Millbank. In this view from the 1920s, the Post Office can be seen on the right, with early petrol pumps in front. It was run by Alf Dickson and Nancy Biggar.

MAINSRIDDLE

So called after Sir James Riddell, Bart, a late eighteenth-century owner of the Southwick estate, this attractive row of cottages has housed a police station, a United Presbyterian Church, a smithy and various shops over the years. It was also the home of *Mainsriddle Man*; a Bronze Age stone coffin was ploughed up in the fields just south of the village in the 1950s, and the remains of both coffin and man can be seen in Dumfries Museum.

HUTLAND, GILLFOOT FARM, SOUTHERNESS
The name Hutland was taken from a 1950s postcard, and was used to describe the curious landscape of wooden buildings ranging from well-built cottages to mere shacks that had grown up on Gillfoot Farm after 1945. They extended almost to the village itself. On the far right the tents show that camping was part of Hutland life; many of the huts were owned by Dumfries and other local folk. A disastrous storm in the early 1960s blew many of the buildings down, and only a few were rebuilt.

JOHN PAUL JONES' COTTAGE

This cottage, in 1747, witnessed the birth of one of Galloway's most ambiguous personalities. To his fellow Scots he was a pirate and traitor, but to millions in the United States, Russia and France he was, and is, a hero. John Paul (he added the Jones later) was the son of a gardener on the Arbigland estate, but embarked upon a colourful naval career after running away to sea as a boy. Known as the founder of the American Navy, he also became a Russian Rear Admiral and a guest of the French revolutionary government. His most notorious local exploit was his raid on the Earl of Selkirk's house of St Mary's Isle, Kirkcudbright when he stole, and later returned, the house silverware.

SOUTHWICK HOUSE

This view shows the mansion in 1915, at the time of Sir Mark McTaggart Stewart's residence. The central part was built in 1750, and the wings were added, along with other improvements, in the late nineteenth century. Sir Mark was known as the *Grand Old Man of Galloway* and was MP for Wigtownshire and the the Stewartry for over twenty years. In the foreground can be seen part of his pedigree herd of Ayrshire cattle. He died in 1923 at the age of 88. The house is now the home of the Thomas family.

CARSETHORN VILLAGE

This tiny village, seen here in about 1960, is just a row of houses fringing the shore where the Nith meets the Solway, but has had an important history. It was the outport for Dumfries for centuries; a cobbled road was built to link the two as far back as the 1660s, and a local mooring was the quarantine station for the Solway from 1710. From the early nineteenth century onwards many thousands of emigrants left Carsethorn for the USA, Canada, Australia and New Zealand and a special jetty was constructed in the 1830s to accommodate the increased traffic. The Steam Boat Inn off the shot to the left is a reminder of the steam packet trade between Carsethorn and Liverpool. The row of two-storey early nineteenth century houses on the left has been home to many retired sea captains.

CARSETHORN, THE *SCOTIA*
The *Scotia* was a trading schooner operating until the early years of last century. This photograph shows it being partly broken up in the 1920s, although the stern remains and still shows occasionally through the sand at low tide.

AIR CHARTER FLIGHT
In June 1947 a party of Southwick men took part in the first charter flight from Dumfries airport, at Heathhall. The trip, to the Isle of Man for the TT Races, was organised by the well-known Dumfries printer and former Guid Nychburris Cornet Mr Eric Grieve. The aeroplane was a De Havilland Dragon Rapide, and the passengers and crew were, from left to right and excluding the flight crew:- Eric Grieve, Alf Dickson, *Ginger* Thomson, A Carruthers, J Connel, Harold Walker, A Thomson. The account of the journey in the Dumfries and Galloway Standard mentions that theirs was one of 150 charter planes at Ronaldsway Airport that day.

SOUTHWICK SCHOOL

The pupils are shown here with their teacher, Miss Begg, in about 1921-2. They are, from left to right:- Back row: Harold Walker, Tom Kyle, John Bell, Jim Ferguson, Willie Drummond, Jim Bell, T. Eaver, ?. Middle row: Rachel Simpson, Maimie Caven, Isa Kelly, ?, Meg McQueen, Lizzie Boddle, Peg Connell, ?. Front row: Addie Thomson, Bessie Carson, May McNaught, Jenny Coltart, ?, Lizzie Thomson, Jean Drummond.

SOUTHWICK TENNIS CLUB
Back row left to right: Robert Thomson, David Foster, Jimmy Thomson, James Kirkland, Herries Clark, John Donaldson, Jim Carson, Beatrice Watson, Margaret Carson. Front row, left to right: Elsie Young, Janet Kirk, Margaret Kirk. The court is still in use just off the back road from Southwick Church to Boreland of Southwick.

CARSETHORN: HARRIS' SHOP
J Harris owned his grocery business by 1887, and had left by 1908. His was one of two shops (both grocers) in the village at the turn of the century; the other was owned by the Stitt family. J Harris was also an innkeeper, and may have run Carsethorn's other pub the *Kings Arms,* which was in existence in 1860.

SOUTHWICK STATION

Was there ever a railway station so wrongly, or maybe optimistically named? Southwick Station was a good, and lonely seven miles from Southwick Church and House, and yet barely two from Dalbeattie on the *Port Road* from Dumfries to Portpatrick. It opened in 1859 and was closed in May 1965, a month before the final and much lamented closure of the whole line. The station building is now a private house.

KIRKBEAN SCHOOL 1917

The pupils and teacher are seen here in a photograph from 1917. Back row, left to right: ? Turnbull, W Stitt, J Cluckie, J Brown, N Oliver, J Stitt, ?, ?. Third row, left to right: Agnes Cluckie, Sally Robson, J Turnbull, Nan Davidson, Molly Stitt, Peggy Cowan, Sally Greig. Second row, left to right: Bessie Robson, Madge Davidson, Mamie Kennon, ? Stitt, Agnes McGhie, Margaret Robson, ?. Front row, left to right: Gavin Turnbull, J Logan, W Wyllie, W Oliver, J W Rae, J Cowan Stitt, H Cowan, T Gordon.

SOUTHERNESS GOLF CLUB
In 1946 Major Richard Oswald began the creation of Southerness Golf Course on land stretching from the village northwards and westwards along the coast. The celebrated golf architect McKenzie Ross was employed as designer, and produced a varied and difficult challenge. Regularly used as a championship course, Southerness was first named in the top fifty courses in Britain by Golf World Magazine in 1988.This recent view shows the clubhouse which was opened in March 1975.

LOANINGFOOT SCHOOL
Loaningfoot School was also known as Preston School, and was about a mile from Southerness. This photograph shows the class of 1914; Nancy Clark, next but one to the left of the boy holding the chalked sign, is the only one still alive, as far as is known.